THE B
GOD'S WORD:
THE EVIDENCE

10 9 8 7 6 5 4 3 2 1
Copyright © 2015 Catherine Mackenzie
ISBN: 978-1-78191-555-4
Published in 2015
by Christian Focus Publications Ltd.
Geanies House, Fearn, Tain,
Ross-shire, IV20 1TW,
Great Britain
Cover design by Daniel Van Straaten
Illustrations by Jeff Anderson
Printed by Bell and Bain, Glasgow

Dedication: With thanks to God for all those who have put
His Word into my life - Grandparents, Parents, Family, Pastors,
Sunday School Teachers and Friends.

THE BIBLE IS GOD'S WORD: THE EVIDENCE

CATHERINE MACKENZIE

CF4·K

A fine and fresh treatment of many key truths about the Scriptures, presented in a way any child can digest. Covering basic hermeneutics, biblical unity, even apparent contradictions and much more, many adult Christians have never learned some of these vital points, and will be pleasantly surprised at how profitable this will be for themselves as they work through it with their children!

Dennis Gundersen
Grace and Truth Books
Oklahoma, U.S.A.

CONTENTS

GET INTO THE PROGRAMME

Let me introduce myself... I'm the Librarian. I've read a lot of books, but I'm here to tell you about the greatest book ever! God's Word: the Bible. However, before we start I want to introduce you to some tools you'll be using as we research this truly amazing book.

When you see this Evidence logo look up the Bible verses. Don't worry if you don't know how to find your way around the Bible. It is, after all, quite a big book. You can use the contents page at the beginning of the Bible to help you. But here's a tip: when you see John 3:16 you need to look up the book of John then chapter 3 and then verse 16. The first word in a Bible reference like this is the book, the first number is the chapter number and the second number is the verse number.

When you see these logos there will be some words and facts to make you sound super intelligent. Trust me, if you drop these words into your conversation, chins are going to drop! You might end up seriously impressing some people! But these words and facts are also useful. For example if you're in the kitchen and you say – 'Put the water in the pan and heat it up to 100 degrees centigrade until the water is bubbling and really, really hot.' That's quite a lot of words. It takes time to say them. But if you know your cooking terms you would just say – 'Boil that water please.' People in the church who have read the Bible use these special words to explain the Bible. It can be fun to learn these words and use them.

And finally, whenever you see the letter **Q:** that's a question someone like you has asked. The people who visit my library are asking them all the time! I'm sure you have loads of questions too.

If there are questions that you still don't know the answers to, after you've read this book, I suggest that you pray to God. Ask him to help you find the answers. And then possibly speak to an older Christian who respects God's Word. Ask them to suggest some more books for you to read. You might end up coming to my library to borrow a few!

GOD AND HIS PLAN

N ow, I hope you're paying attention. The next bit is important, obvious and very easy. The Bible is a book! Got it? Good. Now I'm sure you know what you do with a book? Don't you? Come on? YOU READ IT!!

Word of God/ Bible/ Scriptures. Three names for the same thing: the message that God has given to mankind. It was spoken by God to some of his followers who wrote it down. God used humans to write it, but it is 100 per cent God's Word.

 Psalm 12:6

As well as reading the Bible you've also got to believe it! God's Word is true and it's the greatest book ever!

Q: Why is it the greatest book ever?

That's a good question and the answer is easy. The Bible is the greatest book ever because it is the one book that is written by God.

Q: But who is God?

Ah, another excellent query! God is your creator. He designed the universe in which you live. Everything that lexists has been imagined by him and he made it. The Bible is his message to you. Here are some Bible facts about God to start you off.

1. GOD IS THREE PERSONS IN ONE

The Father, the Son and the Holy Spirit. These three are one God. They are three distinct persons in one God. Each is as glorious as the other and as powerful.

Trinity. This is a word used to sum up God the Father, God the Son and God the Holy Spirit.

About God and the Bible: Matthew 28:19; Genesis 1:26; Isaiah 40:26; Isaiah 43:1; Ephesians 3:14; 1 John 1:1-3; John 1:1; 2 Timothy 3:16; 2 Peter 1:19-21

2. GOD IS A SPIRIT

He doesn't need arms to show his strength. He doesn't need eyes to see, but he did send God the Son to this world to be born with a physical body.

 John 4:24

3. YOU CAN'T MEASURE GOD.

You can't put him in a box, even a very big one or a giant one or one the size of the universe. He wouldn't fit. You can't contain God. You can't put him in a building, or in any kind of space at all and say, 'This is God. That's all there is to him.' No. God cannot be measured.

 **Infinite** (Immeasurable).

Eternal (Forever, Everlasting).

4. GOD IS ETERNAL AND NEVER CHANGES

God has never had a beginning and will never have an end. The God of the olden days and the God of the future is the same God as today. Everything that God is, he has always been and always will be.

 1 Kings 8:27; Psalm 102:12; Hebrews 13:8

5. OTHER CHARACTERISTICS OF GOD

He is wise, powerful, holy, just, good and true. That means he knows everything, is really strong, is perfect and is totally fair. There is nothing bad about him. He does not lie or make a mistake ... he doesn't even think untruths.

Sin: When you do, say or think anything that displeases God, and when you don't do, say or think things that God loves. Sin is anything, that doesn't live up to God's perfect standard. He hates sin.

EVIDENCE

Romans 11:33-34; Jeremiah 32:17; 1 Peter 1:15-16; Psalm 96:13; Psalm 107:8; Psalm 117:2

Q: But why do we need the Bible? What does God want to tell me?

Well, God made us, but human beings rejected God. The first human beings, Adam and Eve, disobeyed God. Human beings have been doing this ever since. The Bible tells us that we are disobedient and sin is highly dangerous.

Q: Why is sin dangerous?

God's law is that sin has to be punished. He hates it because he is perfect. He's not boasting here. It's true. There is not a smidgeon or spot of sin in God. The punishment is serious and must be taken seriously. It is God's eternal, everlasting anger.

Holy (without sin). God is Holy.

We deserve the punishment for our sin. But God has a heart of justice (that must punish sin) and a heart of love that longs to save sinners from that punishment. So that's why we have the Bible. God wants to tell us about his plan to save sinners.

Q: What is the plan?

God's plan to save sinners is throughout the whole Bible. It's everywhere. What a SPLENDID plan it is! I do love it when a plan comes together! You can read about God's plan at the beginning and the middle and the end of the Bible!

 We're sinners. We deserve punishment. God is holy. He hates sin. He must punish it. But he offers us a rescue from sin and punishment. God's Son, Jesus, was born as a human in a town called Bethlehem in the land of Israel. Jesus lived as a human, but without sin. And then he died and was punished instead of sinners. Jesus is fully God and fully man! How unique and amazing is that!

 EVIDENCE   Micah 5:2; Romans 3:23-24

The life that Jesus lived was the perfect life that we can't live. We can't live perfectly, because we are sinners and will never live without sin while we live on this earth. When Jesus died on the cross he took the punishment that our sin deserves. Because he

13

was without sin (holy), he was able to do this. No one else was, or is, or ever will be good enough to do that.

So, because Jesus was without sin and he took the punishment instead, anyone who believes in him is saved from sin. They are forgiven.

Everyone who exists and ever has existed is a sinner—except for Jesus. Eternal punishment is not temporary like a grounding. It's not a ticking off—or being put in the corner. It's a terrible punishment—a death that doesn't end.

Incarnation (God the Son became a human in the womb of Mary).

Crucifixion (Jesus' death on the cross).

Resurrection (raised back to life).Jesus was raised from the dead by the power of God.

John 3:16

That's why you've got to read the Bible! You need to know about this! But there's something more. You've also got to believe it! That's essential! You've got to read it, believe it and obey it!

The Bible is God's Word. It shows us our sin, God, and how God saves. It turns us away from sin, towards God instead. It gives us what we need to believe in him. It changes us and encourages us to be holy.

Repent (turn away from sin).
Salvation (forgiveness of sins).

Q: Is there another book we could read instead? What about other religions?

The Bible, God's Word, is the only way that God communicates with us, so that we can know how to be in a relationship with him.

God is the only true God. Other gods are false idols. The one true God and his Word the Bible is the only truth.

The Bible, the Word of God, is what God uses to turn lives around. All other religions are about man doing his best, but failing, to work his way to heaven. It is the Word of God that transforms sinners, so that they turn away from sin and turn to God instead to have their sins forgiven. It is only by God's love, power and forgiveness that sinners can be saved and obtain eternal life.

It is the power of God's Word that changes the people who believe it and helps them to become holy, like

God. Though they will always battle with sin while they live on this earth, those who believe in God will be made holy and free from sin when they go to heaven. The Word of God is a great comfort when times are hard. It gives us the faith that we need to believe God's Word in the first place!

 EVIDENCE   Acts 20:32

If you have a Bible, read it, or listen to it being read. Prepare yourself. Make sure you don't have any distractions. Before you get into God's Word you need to speak to God himself. Ask him to help you understand what he is saying to you. God's Word is God's way of speaking to you, the person in your skin and your situation! We're to believe God's Word and love it, learn it, treasure it and practise it in our lives!

 EVIDENCE   Psalm 119:18; Psalm 119:11;
James 1: 22-25

Oh! Here's one other question and it's a good one.

Q: What does 'being in a relationship with God' mean?

1. It Means Trust in Him

Because of Jesus' death and resurrection, sinners can be forgiven for their sins and have eternal life. Believing that this is true is being in a relationship with God. That's what trusting in Jesus means.

2. It Means Love Him

We also love God. We love God because he first loved us! God showed his love for us by sending Jesus to die for us while we were still sinners.

 EVIDENCE 1 John 4:19; Romans 5:8

3. It Means Glorify Him

That means we praise him with the words that we say and the actions that we do. We give honour to God and express to others, and to God, how wonderful he is.

4. It Means Enjoy Him

We know how great it is to enjoy things like chocolate or music, sports or movies, family and friends. Being in a relationship with God is something we can enjoy too. God is someone we can enjoy. Being joyful in God means being joyful because of who he is and what he has done for us!

You might notice in this book that I like lists. Numbering things makes me feel organised :-) just in case you're wondering. Now I've got another list for you as we've got some basics that we need to cover before we go too far.

BIBLE BASICS!

The Bible is a book – and I'm sure you've got quite a few of those at home. What kind of books do you like to read? Here are a few of the more common types of books you may have come across:

1. Biographies

These are stories about real life people and what they got up to. Sometimes these are called autobiographies where the person writes about themselves.

The Bible has biographies in it. There are loads of life stories in God's Word. You can read about the life of Joseph who was sold into slavery and then became the ruler of Egypt.

2. Romance

These are stories about when a boy meets a girl, then the girl fancies the boy, and the boy thinks that the girl is gorgeous then the boy and girl get married. (Sigh).

There are romances in the Bible! Yes! Really! Girls meet boys and boys meet girls in this book. There's the story of Ruth, whose husband died but then she went on to marry another godly man, called Boaz. She is in the family tree of King David and Jesus.

3. Poetry

This is when all sorts of interesting descriptive words are used to describe people, nature, history, romance ... anything really. Sometimes the poetry rhymes and often people end up singing it.

David wrote many of the Psalms and his son, Solomon, wrote the Song of Solomon. Moses even wrote a Psalm or two. Some of the songs people sing in church today are based on the Psalms that David wrote.

4. The Past/History Books

These tell you what happened to countries and kings hundreds of years ago.

The Bible is a history book. Read it and you'll find out about lots of historical battles, famines, victories, adventures, kings and queens.

5. The Future/Prophecy

Perhaps you like to read about the past, but then again maybe you want to read about the future. Sometimes there are books written by people who think they know what will happen in the future. But how do we know that's true? We'll have to wait and see.

In the Bible there are books that are called books of Prophecy. This is when God warns his people of their sin and what's going to happen in the future because of that sin. But not all the prophecies are sombre, gloomy warnings – some of them are amazing, full of good news and hope. A lot of the prophecies in the Bible were about the future and the good news that God would send a Saviour one day. When you read about the life and death of Jesus, you will see that loads of the Old Testament prophecies have come true already! In fact, here's an example: Jesus came back to life again after he was killed on the cross.

In the Old Testament, hundreds of years before Jesus rose from the dead, before he died, before he was even born, it was written in the Bible that God's Holy One would not be left to decay in death.

 EVIDENCE Psalm 16:9-10

The Bible prophesied that the Saviour of the world would die, but he wouldn't die forever. His body wouldn't decay in the grave like bodies usually do. It would come back to life. Psalm 16 foretells Jesus' death, resurrection and his ascension (when he returned to heaven). When we see that these prophecies have come true, we can trust that the other prophecies in the Bible will also come true. The Bible tells us that Jesus is going to come back one day.

 Acts 1:11

Because the Bible prophesied that Jesus was going to be born and even prophesied where that would take place, that he was going to die and that he would come back to life—we can be convinced that Jesus is going to come back again some day! The Bible is true!

You see, one of the unique things about the Bible is that it is completely true. The Bible is error free. It's mistake free. It's perfect. There's no other book like the Bible! Because the Bible is God's Word.

 Proverbs 30:5

 **Inerrant** (totally right with no mistakes).

Isn't this utterly amazing? Well, it is God's Word we're talking about! So, yes, the Bible is the greatest book in the world. It is true. It is the Word of God.

GOD WROTE THE BIBLE!

Yes, God did write the Bible, like I said, but it's not just me that's saying it. I didn't invent this. If someone comes to you and says the Old Testament and the New Testament were invented by human beings, well they've got it wrong! Very wrong.

The Bible is divided into two sections – the Old Testament and the New Testament. The Old Testament covers God's story from the time God made the world. The New Testament covers God's story from just before the birth of Jesus, through his life to the start of the church.

Creation (when God made the world).

Q: So it's not true that the Hebrew people invented the Old Testament?

No. It's not true! The history books in the Bible cover real events that happened to the Hebrew people. The Hebrew people were given God's Word but often disobeyed it. They were punished by God and even kicked out of their home country because of their sin.

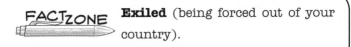

FACTZONE **Exiled** (being forced out of your country).

If you were making up a story about your own country, you'd make sure that your people were the heroes in the book. The Hebrew people aren't really the heroes in the Bible. Sometimes they do the right thing but often, too often, they don't. So the Old Testament is not a Hebrew fiction book.

Q: So what about the New Testament? Some people say that the disciples invented that.

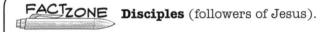

FACTZONE **Disciples** (followers of Jesus).

It's the same thing here as well. When you read about the disciples, you often read about how disobedient they were. Peter often got into trouble. And once he was given the opportunity to stand up for Jesus, but he didn't. So, did guys like Peter and the other disciples invent the story of Jesus? No, because if they had invented the story, they would have made themselves look better.

Q: But I thought some of the disciples did write the Bible?

That's a good point. The Bible has an author – God. He's the one source of inspiration behind all the words you'll see in the Bible. But there are co-authors too. God inspired men, from different times and places and backgrounds, to write the words he wanted them to write. The disciples of Jesus wrote some of the New Testament books: Matthew and John wrote two of the Gospels, Peter wrote two letters or epistles in the New Testament. They would have used a quill and parchment to physically write the words, but in a truly amazing way, God was the one behind every word they wrote.

Q: Were they like puppets then?

No. They weren't puppets or robots either. God gave these writers different talents and styles. If you and I wrote a story about the same subject, we'd write something quite different. That's because we have different personalities and backgrounds. Someone from a cold wet country might complain about a rainy day whereas someone from a desert would write poetry about how he longed for drizzle!

The writers that God chose for the Bible came from different times, countries and languages even. Different perspectives and styles can be seen throughout the Bible—but the message is the same!

 The Old Testament was written in the Hebrew language. The New Testament was written in the Greek language.

God let the writers express themselves, but he inspired them with the words to write. It was as though he breathed the words into them.

So the words in the Bible are God's, but the style belongs to each of the writers. They're not puppets or robots. They're people. They're writers. It's just that there is one primary author behind every one of the writers: God!

 2 Timothy 3:16-17

The Bible is divided up into different sections. There are 39 books in the Old Testament and 27 books in the New Testament. Each book  is divided into chapters and each chapter into verses. The original manuscripts did not have chapters and verses in them. These were added later, so that it was easier to look up a topic or to memorise parts of the Bible.

But even though there are lots of writers, it is a fact that the Bible is God's Word.

The words, 'This is what the Lord says,' or 'Thus says the Lord', occur over 400 times in the Old Testament. The words, 'God said' occur forty-two times in the Old Testament and four times in the New Testament. 'God spoke' appears nine times in the Old Testament and three times in the New Testament.

And we read, several times in the Bible, that God spoke through people.

EVIDENCE   2 Samuel 23:2; 2 Chronicles 20:14

Turn to the next chapter to find out about some of the people God used to write the Bible.

THE BIBLE WRITERS

L et me introduce you to a few of the people God used to write the Old Testament:

Moses: It is generally considered that Moses wrote the first five books in the Old Testament: Genesis, Exodus, Leviticus, Numbers and Deuteronomy. These are history books that also contain God's law.

Law. The Bible contains many laws or instructions from God. God's Word tells us what we should do and what we shouldn't do. If you look in Exodus 20 you will read some of God's law called 'The Ten Commandments'. These were given to Moses on the top of Mount Sinai by God himself. This is one of the rare times in the Bible where we read of God writing something physically himself.

David: Originally a shepherd boy with a talent for music, David eventually became a warrior and the King of Israel. His story is in the historical books of 1 and 2 Samuel, but he wrote many of the Psalms in the book of Psalms. The Psalms are one of the books of poetry in the Bible.

Isaiah: He was a prophet in the Old Testament who often prophesied about the coming Messiah, God's chosen Saviour. He prophesied hundreds of years before Jesus was born. He prophesied that the Messiah would die and that he would save God's people.

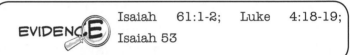

EVIDENCE | Isaiah 61:1-2; Luke 4:18-19; Isaiah 53

Jeremiah: He was a prophet who preached God's message, faithfully warning the people of God about their sin. They often worshipped false gods.

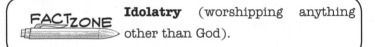

FACTZONE | **Idolatry** (worshipping anything other than God).

Jeremiah had a difficult life. King Jehoiakim took Jeremiah's prophecies and burned them in a fire. But Jeremiah would not stop speaking God's Word. His prophecies came true when King Nebuchadnezzar of Babylon defeated the capital city of Jerusalem and many people were taken captive.

Now let's meet the New Testament writers!

Matthew: He was one of Jesus' disciples. He had another name, Levi. He was originally a tax collector. Tax collectors in New Testament times were not looked on favourably by the people. At that time Israel had been defeated by the Roman empire and tax collectors were looked on as people who sided with the Romans. Matthew wrote his Gospel so that the Jewish people could see that Jesus Christ was King and Messiah ... the Saviour promised by God from the beginning of time.

 EVIDENCE

Ephesians 1:4; Genesis 3:14-15

 FACT FILE

Gospels. Matthew is one of four Gospels in the New Testament. The word 'gospel' means Good News. These four books at the beginning of the New Testament have very good news. In them we see a lot of the Old Testament prophecies coming true through Jesus Christ. The Bible is the Good News of Salvation.

 FACTZONE

Christ. (This is not Jesus' last name – it's another word for Messiah. The word 'Messiah' is Hebrew, the word 'Christ' is Greek. It means Saviour or anointed one.)

Mark: The writer of the Gospel of Mark was not one of the disciples. It's not very clear who he was. He might have been one of Peter's friends. We do know that the book was written with non-Jewish people in mind. The writer of this Gospel wanted people to think about the question 'What did Jesus do?'

Luke: We know more about this writer. He was a doctor and was very detailed in his writing. He wrote the Gospel of Luke and the Book of Acts. He travelled with the Apostle Paul and he witnessed for himself a lot of the stories he wrote about. The Gospel of Luke was written for Greek people and gets us thinking about what Jesus was like. If you want to read why Luke wrote this Gospel turn to Luke 1:1-4 to read this in his own words.

Peter: He was also a disciple of Jesus and wrote two letters or epistles in the New Testament, called 1 Peter and 2 Peter. Even though he denied Jesus, he repented and wept bitterly when he realised what he had done. Jesus reinstated him after the resurrection and Peter went on to be a bold preacher of the Word of God as you can see in the Book of Acts.

Paul: He was known at first as Saul and he started off his story in the New Testament as an enemy of the church. But when he was travelling on the road to Damascus, he came face to face with the risen Lord Jesus. A light blinded him and Jesus spoke to him. Paul realised that he had been fighting against God and God's people. He turned away from his sin and trusted in Jesus Christ.

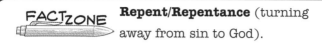

FACTZONE **Repent/Repentance** (turning away from sin to God).

Paul went on to preach the Word of God. He travelled to different countries to do that. New churches sprang up in many of the places he visited. Paul wrote letters to those Christians to teach and encourage them. Many of these are in the Bible, such as 1 Corinthians and Titus.

John: He was one of Jesus' disciples and so was his brother James. It is believed he wrote the Gospel of John, as well as three letters – 1, 2 and 3 John and the Book of Revelation, the last book in the New Testament.

Now we need to dig a little deeper and find out some real evidence for the truth of the Bible and that it is the Word of God!

STRUCTURAL UNITY

So, we know a bit about God, how the Bible was written and why it was written. Now let's look at some of the topics we mentioned earlier, but in greater detail. Let's zone in on the major reasons for why we can say that the Bible is God's Word, that it is true, that it can be trusted.

The first of these reasons is unity.

Q: What do you mean by unity?

Unity means to be one or in agreement. One of the most amazing things about the Bible is its unity. It is so amazing that the Bible's unity can only be explained by the fact that the Bible is God's Word. The unity of the Bible can only be explained by the fact that its origins are divine.

Divine (a word that describes God, or something from God).

Origins (beginnings, source).

Q: So how can I know that the Bible is unified? Can you prove it?

Well, let's start by showing how you might, mistakenly, think that the Bible isn't unified.

1. The Bible is made up of two Testaments, sixty-six books, forty authors and three languages. (Hebrew, Greek and the Aramaic language – a language that was spoken by Jesus and his disciples).

2. The Bible was written over a period of more than 1,500 years.

3. The Bible was written in different countries and cultures by people from different backgrounds, positions in life and careers.

There probably isn't another book anywhere that has been written by kings, poets, fishermen, shepherds and politicians.

King (Solomon), **Poet** (David), **Fisherman** (Peter), **Shepherd** (Amos), **Politician** (Daniel).

Very few of these authors knew each other. They couldn't have sat down together and conspired to fool the world. Most lived in different times, some in different lands ... some wrote poetically, some wrote about history, others gave angry warnings and still others wrote in a loving, tender way. So you could say that the books of the Bible are very different!

Q: What do you mean by structural unity? I don't really understand what that is.

Well, structure means the way the Bible is put together. Even though all these books were written at different times, the Old and New Testaments have a similar format.

The Old Testament begins with a set of books called the Pentateuch – that is Genesis to Deuteronomy. All the other books in the Old Testament build on those. Everything that is taught in the rest of the Old Testament comes from those first books.

It's the same with the New Testament. The first few books, Matthew to John, are the basis of everything else that is taught from Acts to Revelation.

There is history, teaching, devotion and prophecy in the Old Testament and in the New.

The writers of the Bible books didn't sit down and organise this. It just happened this way. That's another piece of evidence to prove that the Bible was written under God's direction. It's divine. God did it!

TESTAMENTS AND UNITY

I have just noticed that another question has come in. It's good to see you're all so inquisitive.

Q: Are the teachings the same in the Old Testament and in the New?

Well, the message is the same, it's just that the Old Testament teaches this message in a different way. Let me explain ... What the Old Testament promises, the New Testament gives.

You see, some of the people we read about in the Old Testament longed to have God's plans revealed to them. They had access to God's law and promises in the Old Testament, but they didn't know how or when God's Saviour would come. They knew and trusted that it would happen, in the future.

In the New Testament we read about how this promised Saviour did arrive, that God himself came to earth. God's Son became a man and lived amongst humanity.

One of the names for Jesus is Immanuel. This means 'God with us'. We read this name first of all in the Old Testament.

Isaiah 7:14

In the Old Testament, prophets foretold that God would send a Saviour. In the New Testament we see that the Saviour arrived in the flesh, Jesus, God's Son.

Q: So are the Old Testament and the New Testament both God's Word? Or does the New Testament replace the Old?

Yes – they are both God's Word, and no, the New Testament does not replace the Old. There is such a remarkable unity between the Old Testament and the New – both must be God's Word.

The New Testament explains the Old Testament. The New Testament often quotes the Old Testament.

Now, here's something you might not have thought of before: The Old Testament was the Bible that Jesus read and quoted in the New Testament.

Q: So the Old Testament was something that Jesus agreed with?

Yes! Here's a couple of things that Jesus said about the Bible. At the time he said these words, the Bible was what we call the Old Testament.

Jesus says that the Law, the Prophets and the Psalms are God's Word. In Luke 24:44-45, Jesus said that all the things written about him in the law and the prophets and the psalms had to be fulfilled.

When you read other things that Jesus said in the

New Testament, you can see that he is using the Old Testament stories in his teaching and that he truly believes that these stories are true.

Luke 11:51 – The story of Abel

Matthew 24:37-39 – Noah

John 8:56-58 – Abraham

Matthew 10:5 – Sodom and Gomorah

Matthew 8:11 – Isaac and Jacob

Matthew 12:39-41 – Jonah

Matthew 24:15 – Daniel

Jesus believed in the Word of God! Nothing that he says is against what we read in God's Word. Jesus warned people that they were not to add to God's Word or take away from it. He quoted the prophet, Isaiah, and said that people should not teach the commands of men as if they were the law of God.

Isaiah 29:13; Matthew 15:9

But there's more to this unity subject. Some people think that the writers in the New Testament disagreed with each other and contradicted each other. Now, do I have to say that that simply isn't true? I suppose I do!

NEW TESTAMENT UNITY

Some people think that the writers of the New Testament can't possibly be in agreement. Some say that one Gospel says one thing and that another of the Gospels says another. That's actually completely wrong, but I see that we have another question here ...

Q: Why are there four Gospels? You say these books agree. So, isn't it a waste of paper and ink to repeat the same stories?

Ah! Here's the answer to that. Although a lot of the stories are the same in the New Testament Gospels, there are different stories too. Take the story of Jesus' birth, for example. Matthew starts with the family tree of Jesus. His book is the only one that tells us about the visit of the Wise Men.

Mark doesn't tell us about Jesus' birth at all, nor does John. But the Gospel of Luke does. Only Luke starts with the story of Jesus' relative, John the Baptist, who was born a few months before Jesus.

So these Gospels aren't needless repetitions, neither are they disagreeing.

Each of the four Gospels tell different parts of the same life story. They're telling this life story from different angles. Each writer wants us to focus on a different aspect of Jesus' biography.

 **Gospel** (the first four books of the New Testament are called Gospels, the word 'gospel' itself means good news. The message of the Bible–salvation and forgiveness of sins–is Good News for sinners).

What Matthew's book focuses on is the fact that Jesus came to fulfil the law and the prophets.

Mark focused on the fact that Jesus came to serve others. He was a humble servant.

Luke focuses on the reason for Jesus coming to the world, which was to save sinners.

And John's purpose for writing his Gospel was to reveal to us that Jesus is God and that we must believe in him.

 Matthew 5:17; Mark 10:45; Luke 19:10; John 1:1-5

All these books are different, but they all agree that Jesus is God, that he saves, that he loves and helps, he is humble and that he fulfilled God's law by keeping it perfectly.

Q: What about the other New Testament writers? Do they agree too?

Well, yes they do. The New Testament has several different writers in addition to the Gospel writers –

and they all agree with each other. However, each of the writers often has a particular topic that they write about.

Paul writes a lot about faith. Peter often writes about hope. John writes about love. James writes about good works. Jude warns about giving up or abandoning your faith.

 **FACT ZONE**   **Apostasy** (to abandon your faith).

Some of these men knew each other, but they could not have sat down together to write these letters. They wrote in different places, to different people, at different times.

The New Testament writers didn't have time to plan with each other what they were writing. They saw a need and did what they could to meet that need. The church in Corinth had to be told where they were going wrong, so Paul wrote a letter. It was the same with the others.

Yet, with all those different letters being sent to all those different people and churches, all the epistles cover all the necessary teaching without any unnecessary overlapping. Remember, there wasn't an editor working away and changing things. It was God who organised it all! So when you look at the Bible and see differences, remember that these differences don't mean disagreements.

The books of the Bible were written to different people, to teach different points. There are different styles and purposes to the different writings, but it is the same message from one God.

The message tells us who God really is and what humans are really like. It warns us that there is one problem: sin and one solution: salvation – through Jesus Christ alone!

This is an important thing to remember: the Bible has a message and it's the same message throughout. And that's what the next chapter is about–unity of message!

MESSAGE UNITY

I have said this before but it's important to keep saying it. The Bible has the same message from beginning to end. Yes! The message of salvation starts in Genesis.

The message of Christ's sacrifice is introduced in the first few chapters of the Bible, because that's when sin raised its ugly head. After Adam and Eve sinned and received the just punishment from God, he gave them a promise. He promised that the evil one would be crushed by one of Eve's descendants. We see Genesis 3:15 fulfilled in Jesus. Jesus' death at Calvary was when he finally defeated the devil and sin. This is also taught in the rest of the New Testament.

 EVIDENCE

Genesis 1 & 2, Genesis 3:15, 2 Corinthians 5:21

 FACT FILE

Adam and Eve sinned against God. They lost their sinless relationship with God through believing a lie told by the devil also known as– the Serpent.

Calvary. This is the place that Jesus was crucified.

So the promise started in Genesis, was fulfilled in the life of Jesus, is taught in the rest of the New Testament and it continues ... The promise will be fulfilled completely in the future, when the devil receives his final punishment from God. This will happen on a day in the future that is called 'Judgement Day'.

 EVIDENCE   Revelation 20:10

Q: What is Judgement Day?

That's a big question. The Judgement Day is the last day, the day when the world and the heavens that God created will be made new. It is when everyone will have to answer to God for the sins they have done. The bodies of those who have died, trusting in Jesus, will be raised back to life, reunited with their spirits and taken to live with God where everything will be perfect and without sin. Sin will be totally removed from the lives of those who have trusted in Jesus and all the horrible things that come with sin will disappear for good ... things like sorrow, death and sickness.

On the Judgement Day punishment will be given to those who have not trusted in Jesus. Those who have not accepted Jesus Christ as their Saviour will be with the devil in Hell. The devil will have no more power or influence.

> **FACTZONE** **Heaven** (the final destination of those who trust in Jesus Christ)
>
> **Hell** (the final destination of those who reject God and Christ's salvation).

The message throughout the Bible is the same. The stories of the Old Testament often help us understand the story of Jesus.

For example, there's the story of Abraham. He was a man who trusted in God and God asked him to sacrifice his son, Isaac. Abraham agreed. When he was about to kill his son on the altar, as a sacrifice to God, the angel of the Lord stopped him, and instead a ram was sacrificed.

When we read of Jesus' death and sacrifice, we realise that it was God the Father who sacrificed his Son. Abraham didn't have to sacrifice his son because God the Son would be the perfect sacrifice for sin.

Throughout the Old Testament, lambs and other animals and birds were used as sacrifices in the temple. The lambs, in particular, were like a picture to help the people see how serious sin was and how it would ultimately be defeated.

49

The lambs were taken to the altar in the temple and killed. Their blood was shed. This showed the people who were watching the sacrifices, and those who read about them later on, that the only way to punish sin was by death. Blood would have to be shed.

But there would never be a little lamb perfect enough to make a perfect sacrifice. Every year a new sacrifice would have to be made. The only one who was good enough to make the perfect, once-for-all, sacrifice was God's Son. Jesus is described in the New Testament as, 'The Lamb of God'.

We also read in Revelation that it was the shedding of Jesus' blood that saves us from sin.

 EVIDENCE   John 1:29; Revelation 5:9

This theme of sacrifice and salvation is like a thread through the whole of the Bible. We read a message of sin and punishment, but also of love and hope when we read the Old and the New Testaments, the prophecies and the poetry and even the romance!

But some people still chose to reject God's Word and say it's full of contradictions. Let's discuss what the best way is to tackle that!

CONTRADICTIONS?

Now I'm sure you've heard that some people say that the Bible contradicts itself by saying one thing and then saying something completely different. If someone comes to you and says that the Bible has contradictions in it, you need to explain to them that it isn't true.

Q: What do you mean by contradiction?

Good question. A contradiction is when two or more statements disagree with each other. They can't both be true.

Take these phrases for example: 'I am going out,' and 'I am not going out'. They can't both be true. However, what about: 'Jane saw three people exit the building' and 'Nick saw two people exit the building'.

These two phrases are different, but can both be true. If Jane was across the street and Nick was around the corner, they were seeing the same place from different angles. Both the phrases can be true.

In the Bible, what people think are contradictions actually turn out not to be! Look at these:

1. Genealogies (Matthew 1 and Luke 3)

Matthew uses a different family tree to Luke. This is not a contradiction. Matthew is using the family of Joseph, Jesus' 'legal' father and Luke traces Jesus' ancestry through the line of Mary, his mother.

2. The Road to Damascus (Acts 9:7 and 22:9)

Did Saul hear a voice or a loud noise on the road to Damascus? Both are referred to. The answer to this conundrum is simple. Those who were with Saul heard the loud noise and it was Saul who heard the voice of Jesus.

3. Matthew Misquotes (Matthew 27:9)

Some people assume that Matthew made a mistake in his Gospel. He quotes Zechariah and says that it was Jeremiah. However, what Matthew does here is merge two quotes. One from Zechariah and one from Jeremiah. He then refers to the prophet Jeremiah as he was the better known. This seems to be an approach used on other occasions, as Mark does something similar when he quotes Isaiah and Malachi.

 EVIDENCE   Mark 1:2-3

So, some of the things that people think are contradictions in the Bible can be explained! The different writers often described the same story from different angles. They saw the same event, but different parts of it.

If someone does ask you about contradictions in the Bible, ask them what these contradictions are. They may just be repeating something they heard someone else say, or they may have misunderstood what the Bible is saying.

It can be easy to make a mistake, if you just read a verse and not all the other verses round about it. Find an older Christian who loves the Word of God. Ask them to read the Bible with you and your friend. It's a good idea if you have another Christian or Pastor with you to help answer your friend's questions. It will help your friend and perhaps you to understand what God is really saying in his Word.

Next we're going to quickly look at another reason the Bible is God's Word. It has authority and power.

AUTHORITY AND POWER

So what we're talking about here is that the Bible is God's Word and that we can trust it … we can believe that it is really true. It has the power to change lives and save souls! It's reliable and can be trusted.

Soul (The spiritual part of you that believes in God or doesn't).

Q: How can I really believe God's Word is true?

Believing God's Word to be true is something that really only God can help you do. You should ask him to help you believe his Word.

 Mark 9:24

Authority (reliability, can be trusted).

Q: So, how can I rely on the Bible? How can I be confident in it?

Well, if you bought a cookery book or a 'How to mend your broken bike' book – what would persuade you that it was a good book to start with? What would persuade you that this was a book you needed on your shelf? Well, maybe you don't cook or ride a bike, but often books like this will have someone endorse the book. That means there are people who have read the book and know that it does what it says. 'I used this book and now I cook like a professional chef!' They might say something like, 'The tyres were bust, the bell didn't work and every time I rode my bike I had an accident. Those days are gone! Next year I'm going to win the Tour de France!'

These are good endorsements and the Bible has endorsees too! For example, Paul wrote in Corinthians that the Bible has been given to us by God. And Paul wasn't just speaking about the Old Testament, he was referring to the New Testament too.

The Bible is also endorsed by Jesus Christ! Now, you have to pay attention to what he says!

Jesus believed that the writers of the Old Testament were inspired by God, and that we must believe what Moses wrote and what he, Jesus, says.

 **EVIDENCE**

1 Corinthians 2:9-10;
1 Corinthians 2:12-13;
1 Corinthians 14:37; Mark 12:36
and Psalm 110:1; John 5:47

So, Jesus is saying that we must believe the Old

Testament. Remember how Jesus quoted from the Old Testament history books and that he believed that these people such as Abel, Noah and Jonah were real. He also believed the Old Testament prophecies. He often quoted them in his teaching.

Matthew 11:9-10 and Malachi 3:1 (About John the Baptist).

Matthew 26:31 and Zechariah 13:7 (Jesus talking about his own death).

John 13:18 and Psalm 41:9 (Jesus talking about how he would be betrayed).

Jesus endorsed the Old Testament Scriptures by saying that they were written about him.

Jesus also endorsed his own words. He was certain that his words were true. He said that his words were eternal and that they would set people free. He declared that the words he spoke were straight from God the Father and that they were life-giving.

Matthew 26:24; John 5:39, Mark 13:31; John 8:31-32; John 7:16; John 12:49; John 6:63; John 5:24.

Jesus also endorsed the words of his followers – even though they didn't write the New Testament until after Jesus had returned to heaven.

Ascension (describing how Jesus returned to heaven by rising up in a cloud).

Jesus declared that the words of his followers would also be words from God and that they should be believed in the same way that people should believe his own words.

Jesus had, in fact, given the disciples the same words and message that God had given him.

Jesus stated that, in the future, God would give his followers the right words to say.

John 16:12-13; Matthew 10:14; Luke 10:16; John 17:8; Mark 13:11; Matthew 10:20

Do you find all this as amazing as I do? Isn't it remarkable? We're going into an even more fascinating subject next: Prophecy!

PROPHECY

We need to start this part with a brief reminder of what prophecy is.

Q: Isn't prophecy just about telling what's in the future?

That's only part of it. Prophecy in the Bible is a message from God. He put this message into the mouths and thoughts of men that he had chosen and this message was passed on to God's people.

God's People – in the Old Testament these words referred to the Hebrews or Jewish people, the nation God had chosen to be his people and to give his Word to. The words 'God's People' now refer to all those who believe in Jesus Christ as God's Son and the promised Saviour.

Prophecy in the Bible was written or spoken by the prophets and given to God's people sometimes as a warning and sometimes as an encouragement. God wanted to warn them of the consequences of their sin, but he often wanted to give them a message of hope too, that one day sin would be defeated.

However, these prophecies were not just written for the people of Bible times. They were written so that God could pass on that same message to his people in the future. So, today when we read these prophecies, God is speaking to us, and in the future when people who haven't even been born yet, read God's Word, God will speak to them too.

Q: Could these prophets be trusted?

There were false prophets who pretended to speak God's Word. However, the prophets whose words are recorded in the Bible can be trusted. They were spokesmen for God and the Bible is strict about how to test whether a prophet is true or false.

The people were to read God's Word and if what the prophet said did not agree with what God said that false prophet was to be killed. So both God and his Word take prophecy seriously.

 EVIDENCE   Deuteronomy 13:5

Q: How do we know that the prophecies were real? They may have been written about the times they were living in and not about the future at all?

I'm so glad you asked that! We are talking about hundreds of prophecies here. Do you realise that? Hundreds of prophecies from the Old Testament have come true. It's really quite spectacular! These prophecies have come true a lot of times through Jesus Christ. These prophecies were definitely not written at the time Jesus was alive. They were in fact written hundreds of years before he was even born!

 Genesis 3:15 and Galatians 4:4

Here are some other prophecies that were fulfilled by Jesus Christ.

1. The Promised Saviour would be in the family tree of Shem, Abraham, Isaac and Jacob.

 Genesis 22:18; Genesis 26:2-4; Genesis 28:13-14

These prophecies were fulfilled in the family tree of Jesus that we read in the New Testament.

 Luke 3: 34-36; Matthew 1:1

2. The Promised Saviour would be of the nation of Israel, the tribe of Judah and the family of Jesse.

 Deuteronomy 18:18; Genesis 49:10; Isaiah 11:1-2

These prophecies also came true in the life of Jesus.

EVIDENCE — Romans 9:4-5; Hebrews 7:14; Matthew 1:6

In fact, once you start looking at how many prophecies came true through the life and death of Jesus Christ, it's quite staggering!

Here are some of the prophecies fulfilled through Jesus' birth and life.

1. The Promised Saviour would be born of a Virgin

EVIDENCE — Isaiah 7:14

We read in Matthew's Gospel that Mary was a virgin and that she conceived Jesus through the power of the Holy Spirit. This is why God is the only true Father of Jesus Christ. Joseph was not his real father.

EVIDENCE — Matthew 1:18-23; Luke 3:23

2. The Promised Saviour was to be born at Bethlehem

EVIDENCE — Micah 5:2

Bethlehem was where Joseph took Mary for the census when she was pregnant with Jesus and this is where she gave birth to him.

 Matthew 2:1-8

3. The Murder of the Infant boys

This is a tragic story of how Herod orders the deaths of all infant boys in Bethlehem of two years old and under. He was attempting to kill the child Jesus who he feared would take his throne from him. This event was also prophesied in the Old Testament.

 Jeremiah 31:15; Matthew 2:16-18

4. The Escape to Egypt

It was prophesied in Hosea that the promised Saviour would be in Egypt at some point. That was where Jesus and his parents escaped to when the angel warned Joseph in a dream about Herod's plot.

 Hosea 11:1; Matthew 2:12-15

5. Galilee

The fact that Jesus would spend time in Galilee and have a healing ministry was also prophesied. Many times in the Gospels we read about how this took place.

Isaiah 35; Matthew 8; Isaiah 9:1-2; Matthew 4:15-15

But it's not just Jesus' birth and life that were prophesied about. The prophets declared that the Saviour would die for our sins, and be sold for thirty pieces of silver, be betrayed, spat upon, whipped, crucified, rejected, forsaken by God, have his hands and feet pierced ... And there's more ... People would gamble for his clothes, none of his bones would be broken and he would pray for his enemies. All of these were prophesied in the Old Testament and it all happened during the crucifixion of Jesus. Read the following Bible Evidence—it's fascinating!

Isaiah 53:8; 2 Corinthians 5:21

Zechariah 11:13; Matthew 27:3-4

Psalm 41:9; John 13:18-21

Isaiah 50:6; John 18:22

Isaiah 53:5; John 19:1

Deuteronomy 21:23; 1 Peter 2:24

Isaiah 53:3; 1 Peter 2:4-8

Psalm 22:1; Matthew 27:46

Psalm 22:16; John 20:27

Psalm 22:18; John 19:23-24

Psalm 34:20; John 19:33-36

There were prophecies too about what would happen after Jesus' death.

1. A rich man named Joseph took Jesus' body to his own tomb for burial. The prophet Isaiah foretold that the Saviour's burial place would be with the rich.

 Isaiah 53:9; Matthew 27:57-60

2. In the Psalms it was foretold that the promised Saviour's body would not decay and we know that three days after his death, Jesus came back to life.

 Psalm 16:10; Acts 13:35

Ah... I see an extra question has come in.

Q: Do we know the resurrection is true?

Well, we're going a bit off course here, but it's an important question and one I think I should deal with straight away! It is, after all, something that shows God's Word is true.

The resurrection is true and not a made up story because...

1. Women are the first witnesses of the resurrection. If it had been a made up fictional account that would have been different. In those historic times a woman's testimony did not have the same value as a

man's. But God chose women to be the first people to see the risen Lord Jesus. Although the people in Bible times might have been more inclined to believe the account of a man, today these particular details help us to believe that the Bible is actually true. If the story of the resurrection was made up then the writers would have written about men rather than women finding the tomb empty!

2. There are loads of eye witness accounts. Women, men and at one point even more than 500 people at once saw the risen Lord Jesus.

 1 Corinthians 15:3-8

3. Some people say that not only did Jesus not rise from the dead, he didn't even die on the cross. Really, those are total lies! There were eye witnesses of that event too. The disciple, John, was there, Mary, his mother, and other women.

 John 19:25-27

4. Other eye witnesses of the crucifixion were the Roman soldiers. They made sure Jesus was dead. They checked! And double-checked. That was their job. They knew if someone was dead or not. If they made a mistake and said that someone was dead when he wasn't, they would be killed for it.

5. The soldiers broke the legs of the criminals on either side of Jesus. These two men were still alive. Breaking their legs made them die more quickly. But when they came to Jesus, they discovered that he was dead already. So they didn't break his legs, but to be on the safe side one soldier took a spear and pierced Jesus' side with it. Blood and water gushed out. This is a physical reaction that only happens when a person's body is dead. The Roman soldiers were convinced – their captive had been killed.

EVIDENCE John 19:33-37

So, eyewitness accounts are important. In a court room they are vital when presenting evidence. The eye witness accounts are the backbone to the evidence about Jesus' death and resurrection.

Bible Manuscripts. It is widely supported that the Gospels Matthew, Mark and Luke were written twenty to thirty years after Jesus' resurrection. John's account was probably written seventy years after the events. Paul's letter to the Corinthians was written twenty-five years after Jesus' death. Because all these books were written so close to the events they recorded, we know that the writers still had a clear memory and access to the memories of many people who had actually witnessed the events.

THE TEMPLE

In the Old Testament we read about the Temple. We learn about the festivities and special offerings that happened during the Hebrew calendar. The temple and the objects inside it were a way that God showed his people what the promised Saviour would be like. The festivities and offerings were tools he used to teach the people about sin and forgiveness.

Q: What's the temple?

The temple was the place where God's people went to worship God. Originally it was a tent, but later on, King Solomon built a more permanent structure, a house for the Lord, and it was called the Temple.

Worship (to honour God through prayer, singing and devotion).

In the temple there was a holy place called 'The Holy of Holies'. This was where the High Priest went once a year to seek God's forgiveness for the nation's sin. Inside was a special box called the 'Ark of the Covenant'. And certain parts of the ark were visual prophecies about Jesus Christ.

1. The ark was made out of wood. This was a picture that showed the Saviour would be human.

2. The ark was covered with gold. This showed that the Saviour would also be God.

3. The ark also had a lid on it made of pure gold. This was called 'The Mercy Seat'. On a special day in the Hebrew calendar called 'The Day of Atonement', the High Priest would enter *The Holy of Holies* and sprinkle blood on *The Mercy Seat*. This was a prophecy, a foretelling of Christ's sacrifice.

 EVIDENCE   1 Timothy 3:16; Exodus 37:1-9

Throughout the year in the temple different offerings were made. Here are two of them...

1. Burnt Offerings. These were voluntary offerings and were to be faultless. Everything was to be burnt up on the altar.

 EVIDENCE   Leviticus 1:3 and 9; Hebrews 9:14

The burnt offering was a foretelling that Jesus would be the perfect sacrifice and that he would willingly give himself and hold nothing back.

2. Sin Offerings. For this offering a bullock, young goat or lamb without any fault was chosen for the sacrifice. The person making the offering lay his hand upon the head of the animal. The animal was a substitute for them. Their sin was transferred onto the animal. The body of the animal that had been killed was then taken outside of the city and burned there.

 **Substitute** (Someone that takes the place of another).

This offering was a foretelling of how Jesus would be killed outside the city, as a substitute for sinners.

 Leviticus 4:20; 2 Corinthians 5:21; John 1:29

God instructed the Hebrew people to have special celebration days throughout the year. I'll just mention two of them here. There were, in fact, quite a few which must have made the year enjoyable. But these two festivities were actually quite serious as well...

1. The Passover. This was first celebrated when the Hebrew people were slaves in Egypt. Pharaoh kept forbidding the people to leave. He would not set God's people free. God sent plagues on the land, but did not send them on the part of Egypt that the Hebrews lived in. The last plague was the worst by far. It was the plague of death. The Hebrew people were given instructions to paint blood on the tops and sides of their doors. It was to be the blood of a lamb. Then the people were to have a special meal of roast lamb, bitter herbs and unleavened bread (bread with no yeast in it). Later, when the angel of death came over the land, he passed over those homes that had blood painted on their doors. No one died in these families. But every Egyptian home was visited by death that night. Every first born Egyptian child perished. Because lambs had been killed that night Hebrew families had been saved. The Hebrew people remember that night, every year, by having the same meal of lamb, herbs and bread.

The death of the lambs that night was a foretelling of what Jesus would do to save sinners. Remember, he is called 'The Lamb of God'. He died so that sinners could live eternally.

 EVIDENCE   Exodus 12; John 1:29; John 3;16

2. The Day of Atonement. There was one day, every year, when the whole nation of Israel was cleansed from their sin. Two goats were chosen. The sins of the people were transferred onto one of the goats. That goat was led out into the wilderness to die. The people's sins were being taken away by God and would be forgotten. The other goat was killed and the High Priest took the blood into *The Holy of Holies* and sprinkled it on *The Mercy Seat*. The nation's sin was atoned for.

This was a foretelling of how Jesus Christ would die to redeem his people.

Atonement (When something is done to make amends for wrong doing. When humanity is reconciled to God through the death of Christ.)

Redeem (to buy back, take back).

Leviticus 16; Hebrews 9:12

So, after all that I think it might be worthwhile looking at some of the other evidence that's around to support that the Bible is God's Word and is true.

Have you ever heard of archaeology?

OLD TESTAMENT ARCHAEOLOGY

A rchaeology is really the study of ancient cultures by the scientific analysis of physical remains. I know, that sounds pretty intelligent, doesn't it? I told you people would be impressed with you after you'd read this book ... but what's this? Another question! Great!

Q: I don't understand what you're saying. Please simplify.

Oh well, I suppose I should. You've seen archaeologists on TV probably, and in books. They spend a lot of time digging around in the ground because, over the centuries, the ordinary bits and pieces of life, like pots and pans, money, buildings and the like, crumble to pieces and end up being covered by soil and dirt. When these objects are dug up by the archaeologists they look at them in detail and learn a lot about the time these objects were from and the people who used them.

Sometimes they even dig up historical writings such as tablets of stone or scraps of leather. The evidence that they've discovered from digging up engravings, from these historical civilisations, such as Egypt and Babylon, actually back up a lot of the Bible accounts.

So, it's a fascinating subject to study. Unfortunately, some archaeologists do not believe that the Bible is true. Some have decided that if there is no archaeological proof that the Bible accounts actually happened, then they can't be true. But true archaeology is always discovering new cities, new cultures, new artefacts. ... and that's what has happened! And surprise, surprise, a lot of the new discoveries actually prove that the Bible writings have been true all along. Let me show you some examples ...

1. Abraham/Patriarchal History. Abraham was the one chosen by God to start the new nation of the Hebrew people. He left his home city of Ur of the Chaldeans to live in the land of Canaan.

Some people who studied the time of the Patriarchs i.e. the time of Abraham, Isaac and Jacob – used to think that Abraham was a legend or myth. However, opinions have changed. Archaeologists now agree that the biblical account of Abraham is accurate.

It has been reported that over 100,000 clay tablets have been dug up from this time period by archaeologists. These writings and the Bible accounts match up remarkably.

Abraham's story is very like the other stories and customs that archaeologists have discovered from that area.

Common Customs: Adoption

Childless couples would adopt a boy who would then inherit their wealth.

The Bible tells us the story of the childless Abraham and Sarah. Abraham chose to have a man Eliezar as his heir, but in the end, when Isaac was born, it was no longer necessary to do this.

Heir (Someone who is given or inherits the possessions of a parent or person who has died).

Common Customs: Working for a Wife

Another common practice during those times was for a servant to work for a certain amount of time for his master and then at the end of his contract he would be given a wife. Jacob did exactly this. In fact, he worked for a total of fourteen years in order to get the woman he loved.

Common Customs: Family Idols

Many people from Abraham's original home in Ur worshipped idols at that time. They often had their own set of family idols. Whoever had those idols in their possession was considered to be the head of the family. In the Bible we read the story about Jacob's wife, Rachel, stealing her father's family idols. Laban, her father, was anxious to get them back to pass them on to his sons. Instead Rachel hides them away for herself and her husband. She may have wanted to have the family power and wealth for her own husband and children.

Here's some other archaeological evidence that matches the Bible.

2. Abraham and his Ancestors. In Joshua 24:2 we read that Abraham and his ancestors lived on the other side of the river Euphrates and worshipped other gods.

For centuries, no one knew where the city of Ur was. It had been buried under the ground and over the years people had forgotten all about it. However, today the city of Ur is one of the best known archaeological sites of southern Babylon, right where the Bible says it is! So much information has been discovered about this city, its buildings, government and wealth. The people definitely worshipped other gods, as a place of worship has been discovered called a Ziggurat. This place was devoted to the worship of the moon god. A whole quarter of the city was given over to the worship of this false god. So moon worship was a huge part of the city's life.

This proves that the Bible was right again—Abraham did come from the other side of the Euphrates and his ancestors worshipped other gods. This is another example of how archaeology supports the truth of the Bible.

It should make us think twice if we ever hear of archaeological discoveries that claim to disprove the Bible. It's more than likely they've made a mistake. It will be the archaeologists that are wrong not the Bible.

Q: But perhaps people added all these details to the Bible later, just to make everything look good.

No! That didn't happen. Remember we discussed it earlier on. The writers just couldn't have sat down and edited the Bible. Everything looks like it has been written by one author because it actually has been ... by God! And when we're talking about archaeology – so much of the archaeological evidence that we have today was not available to the Bible writers. This information has only come to light hundreds of years after the Bible was written. It would have been impossible for the people who wrote the Old Testament to

have access to all the information that we have access to today.

Scientists and archaeologists who know about these ancient cultures and who read the biblical account of Abraham agree that the Bible story is not made up.

3. Joseph and Pharaoh. Here's another interesting piece of archaeological evidence. Do you remember the story of Joseph, how he was sold into slavery by his brothers and then rose up to become a prominent ruler in the land of Egypt?

There have been excavations done in Egypt that support the story of Joseph as we read it in the Bible.

Egyptian artists created murals and paintings during the times of the Pharaohs. These illustrations showed a ceremony taking place – one where a ruler was being presented before the people. This ceremony is called an 'investiture' today.

The Egyptian artists accurately depicted the way that Pharaoh honoured Joseph in the Bible story we read in the book of Genesis.

4. The Invasion of Canaan. An ancient letter has been discovered, written by the King of Jerusalem before the Hebrew people took over the land of Canaan. In his letter the king says, 'The Habiru have wasted all the territory.' This is now seen as evidence supporting the fact that the Hebrew people, also known as the Jews, invaded the land of Canaan. We read about this in the books of Exodus and Joshua.

However, we also read in the Bible that the invasion of Canaan didn't happen overnight. It was gradual.

 Joshua 13:1

Archaeological digs have shown that this is true. They have worked out through scientific investigation that certain towns were destroyed by the Hebrew people at certain times. But that other towns withstood the invasion until years later.

5. King Belshazzar. And then this next piece of evidence is fascinating! For some time archaeologists disagreed with the Bible when the book of Daniel said that Belshazzar was king at the time of the fall of Babylon.

 Daniel 5

Archaeologists believed that Nabonidus was the ruler at that time. Certain ancient documents and records said this – so they assumed that the Bible was wrong! But, later on, further evidence was brought to light.

Nabonidus and Belshazzar were co-rulers for the last part of Nabonidus' reign. When Nabonidus was in Arabia he let his eldest son, Belshazzar, rule instead.

Sorted!

But it's not just the Old Testament that archaeology backs up, it's the New Testament too. But that's for the next chapter.

ARCHAEOLOGY AND THE NEW TESTAMENT

Archaeology supports what we read in the New Testament too. People have done historical research, reading a lot of the ancient documents that date from the same time. There have been excavation digs at Corinth, Athens and Philippi that show how the Bible stories connected to these places are accurate.

But again people still think that the Bible has got it wrong. One example of this is how people thought that Luke had made some mistakes in his writing. Now that was silly. Everything about Luke shouts out 'accurately written detail!' Yet again the Bible was proven to be true – and the critics mistaken!

You see, Luke had given some geographical details in his account. He had mentioned that Iconium was in Phrygia.

People disagreed about this and then a document was discovered which showed that Luke had been right. The city of Iconium was governed by the area of Galatia, but the whole city actually spoke the language of Phrygia. Because of that Luke was right to refer to the city as Phrygian!

Case solved!

In fact there are loads of historical documents that can be researched and used as evidence to support the New Testament.

Many events recorded in the Bible are referred to elsewhere, on the walls of palaces, in letters and journals of people who did not write in the Bible or under God's inspiration. However, they can still be read and used by people who believe the gospel – as they are evidence that the Bible events did occur.

The existence of Jesus Christ is recorded by several historians of that period.

Q: Who exactly?

Well, let me introduce you to them: Josephus, Suetonius, Thallus, Pliny the younger and Lucian.

Q: So why isn't their material included in the Bible? I think I've heard of other books that weren't put into the Bible?

You will have. Quite a lot of interest has sprung up recently about some of these books. But the early church was very strict about what books and writings made it into the Bible.

Canon of Scripture (the authentic writings to be included in God's Word).

To get into the Canon of Scripture the book had to be written by an apostle, someone who had seen the risen Lord Jesus. Or the book could be written by someone who was very close to an apostle.

The writings had to agree with God's Word.

The books excluded by the early church did not match up to their exact standards – the standards of God and his Word.

Q: What about the times after the Bible was written? Is there historical proof to support that they didn't let mistakes creep into the Bible?

Well, I suppose there is. You see the Bible has been passed on from generation to generation. God hasn't just inspired Scripture, he has ensured that it has been passed on correctly too. He has divinely inspired scripture and made sure that it is remembered and written correctly.

History shows us that the Bible has been written out meticulously! The pages were copied by professional writers called scribes. Being a scribe was a full-time job. They did their work very, very carefully. It was God's Word after all and they deeply respected it.

Q: How carefully did they copy it?

I did say 'very carefully' didn't I? Well historians know exactly how these ancient scribes copied out Scripture.

The Jews and early Christians so respected the Word of God they took unusually great care over it. They had special clothes to wear! I mean— that's how important they thought it was. The ink was made to a particular recipe. The Jewish scribes had to say each word aloud when they were writing and each time they wrote the name of God they had to wash their pens and their bodies!

Q: So how did they ensure that there were no errors or mistakes?

Well, every time a page was copied they had to check it against the original. Every word was checked, again and again ... and again!

Not even a letter could be written down from memory. So a scribe was constantly checking his work as he went along. He even had to count how many letters were on each page! Yikes! The first word of every line and the middle word of each page was checked.

Then the chief scribe rechecked everything once more.

Each scribe wrote their page in columns. Each column was never fewer than forty-eight lines and never more than sixty lines.

If the scribe made even one mistake, the whole page was destroyed. No mistakes were allowed to stay in the system, just in case someone copied a mistake. It could not be allowed to even exist on paper.

Once a manuscript was completed it had to have a final check within thirty days. If three pages needed corrections the whole manuscript had to be redone.

Now, it is because of God's power and his influence over the minds of the biblical writers that we have the Bible. But he has also influenced the minds and the pens of those people who recorded scripture. That is one reason why we can trust the Bible and its accuracy. From the very first word that was breathed into the mind and pen of the first prophet, through the choices that the

early church made regarding the Canon of Scripture, right through to today– God has preserved his Word.

Today, we have the Bible in our language, accurate and inspired because of God's power. Today, the Bible is being translated throughout the world for people who do not even have a small portion of God's Word in their own language ... yet!

God's work and his Word continues.

So let's leave the last word in this book to the Bible, God's Word!

THE LAST WORD IS THE BIBLE'S

This is what the Bible says about itself. This is what the Bible says it is like.

A Sword: The Bible describes itself as a sword because like a sword it is sharp and powerful. A sword can cut and pierce. The Bible, God's Word, can cut away at all the sin in our lives. Sometimes we want to stand up to the Bible and stop it doing what it does best. Sinners don't want to listen to God's Word telling them that they deserve to be punished for sin. But God's Word cuts through that armour. In the end there is nothing that can stop God's Word. When God has decided that someone should hear his Word and believe it—his Word will accomplish that!

 Ephesians 6:17; Hebrews 4:12

A Hammer: This is a useful tool. It smashes things and can be used to build things. God's Word destroys evil plans. Sin has no power against the Word of God. But it builds up a life of love and obedience to God.

 Jeremiah 23:29

A Mirror: When you look in a mirror you see what is there. You see where you are. It's reflected back at you. The mirror shows you if there is any toothpaste smeared across your face! When you look in the Bible it shows you your sin. But it does more than that—the mirror of the Bible shows us who to go for forgiveness of our sin—Jesus Christ.

 James 1:23-25

A Lamp: On a dark night we need a lamp or a torch to show us the way ahead. Sometimes people have a torch on their mobile phones these days. A light keeps us away from danger in the dark. The Bible has been given to show us the way to salvation. It guides us away from the danger of sin to the safety of Jesus Christ.

 Psalm 119:105

Water: We use water to clean things. We also use it when we are thirsty. When God's Word changes a person, it is like they are being washed clean of their sin. You start to see sin being replaced by things that please God. The Bible also gives life and refreshment to someone who believes God and his Word. A cool drink on a hot day is great. God's Word also gives us great joy as it encourages us and strengthens us to do what God wants us to do.

 Ephesians 5:26 and John 15:3

Gold: We'd all like to find a chest of gold. Gold is valuable. If you found a stack of it you would be very rich indeed! The Bible is very valuable. There is no other book that gives the great news of how to get eternal life!

 Psalm 19:9-10

And this is what the Bible says its does.

- The Word of God teaches us and corrects us. (2 Timothy 3:16).

- The Word of God encourages us and gives us hope. (Romans 15:4).

- The Word of God will last forever. (Isaiah 40:8).

- The Word of God gives us life. (John 6:63).

- The Word of God fights against sin. (Psalm 119:11).

- The Word of God judges us. (John 12:47-48).

- The Word of God saves our souls. (James 1:21).

THE BIBLE IS GOD'S WORD

So I suppose the final question is min
have, after all, been answering rathe
lot of questions in this book. So here
then...

Are you willing to accept that
Bible is true, that it is the Wor
God and that it is the only way
you to know God and his pla
salvation?

Do you see that what the E
tells you, about yourself, is tr

You are a sinner. You need salva
You cannot be forgiven by Goc
obtain eternal life by working fo
Your good works are not good enc
for that. Eternal life is not something
can buy. In fact, you can't even bel
in God unless he gives you faith. But
does that—he gives us faith, he give
eternal life—as a free gift!

He devised a plan to save sinners f
sin and eternal punishment. He
his Son, Jesus Christ, to liv
perfect life as a man and then to
on the cross—taking the punishr
that sinners deserve for their sin.

Can you see that this is true?

If not, ask God to make you see.

His Word is the most important book in the world, ever. You need to believe it! Do you? That's the question and that's the challenge!

Till next time!

● ●

BIBLIOGRAPHY

The following books were used along with the Bible in the research and thinking behind this book.

Downey, Peter and Shaw, Benn, *Everything you want to know about the Bible*, Zondervan, 2005

Lawson, Roderick *Shorter Catechism*, Christian Focus Publications, 2007

Orr-Ewing, Amy, *But is it real?*, Inter-Varsity Press, 2008

Orr-Ewing, Amy, *Why Trust the Bible?*, Inter-Varsity Press, 2005

Peckham, Colin, *The Authority of the Bible*, Christian Focus Publications, 1999

Stott, John, *Contemporary Christian*, Inter-Varsity Press, 1992

Wells, Paul, *Taking the Bible at Its Word*, Christian Focus Publications, 2013

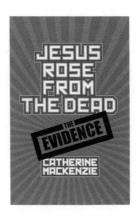

If you were to go out into the street with a questionnaire to find out what people thought about truth you would get a variety of answers. Some people think that the truth doesn't really matter. They think it's all right for one person to believe one thing and another person to believe something entirely different.

Sadly many people today instead of believing the truth about Jesus Christ, actually believe the lies that are told about him.

So what do you believe about Jesus Christ? Do you believe he rose from the dead? This book will help you find out the truth - and how this truth is not only amazing - it also makes sense!

Isbn: 978-1-84550-537-0

"I think it is an excellent approach

and one much needed"

John Blanchard ~ Internationally known Christian preacher, teacher, apologist and author

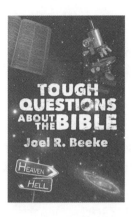

Have you ever asked "Why did God allow Adam and Eve to sin? Why did he create mosquitoes? What is God's plan for me?" Sometimes we have really tough questions about life, about death, even about God.

Children from a variety of backgrounds have come up with the questions in this book and Joel Beeke has done his best to answer these in the light of God's Word. These are real questions from real children in real life situations - and a real pastor with a genuine concern for their souls takes them to the one true God and the real gospel.

Isbn: 978-1-78191-230-0

"Kids ask the toughest questions and who hasn't been caught wondering how to answer? I can think of no one better to answer the toughest of questions than Joel Beeke. "
Derek Thomas ~ Senior Minister of Preaching and Teaching, First Presbyterian Church, Columbia, South Carolina

"This book will provide a useful tool in family worship or daily reading."
Simonetta Carr, Author

CHRISTIAN FOCUS PUBLICATIONS

Christian Focus | Christian Heritage | CF4K | Mentor

Christian Focus Publications publishes books for adults and children under its four main imprints: Christian Focus, CF4K, Mentor and Christian Heritage. Our books reflect our conviction that God's Word is reliable and Jesus is the way to know him, and live for ever with him.

Our children's publication list includes a Sunday School curriculum that covers pre-school to early teens, and puzzle and activity books. We also publish personal and family devotional titles, biographies and inspirational stories that children will love.

If you are looking for quality Bible teaching for children then we have an excellent range of Bible stories and age-specific theological books.

From pre-school board books to teenage apologetics, we have it covered!

Find us at our web page:
www.christianfocus.com

CF4•K
Because you're never
too young to know Jesus